A Teacher's Guide to CREATING PORTFOLIOS

For Success in School, Work, and Life

MARTIN KIMELDORF

EDITED BY PAMELA ESPELAND

free spirit
PUBLiSHiNG®

Works for kids®

Cover and book design by MacLean & Tuminelly

Index prepared by Eileen Quam and Theresa Wolner

10 9 8 7

Printed in the United States of America

The Talents Poster Exercise on pages 49–54 has been adapted from *Write Into a Job* by Martin Kimeldorf, with permission of the publisher, Meridian Education Corporation. These pages are reproducible for classroom use only.

FREE SPIRIT PUBLISHING INC.
217 Fifth Avenue North, Suite 200
Minneapolis, MN 55401-1299
(612) 338-2068
help4kids@freespirit.com
www.freespirit.com

Acknowledgments

I would like to thank all of the contributors to this teacher's guide, and especially my editor at Free Spirit Publishing, Pamela Espeland. Her uncommon common-sense approach to editing has added great value to this guide.

Contents

....

Foreword

....

"What do you picture when you hear the word 'portfolio'? Maybe you think of an artist's case, a ring binder, a scrapbook, drawstring bag, shoe box, or manila folder. Some students fashion their own containers, pouring as much imagination into the holder as into the contents. In truth, any portfolio exists first and foremost in the heart and mind of the designer, who selects with care those works and artifacts that best tell the story of who that person is now—and who he or she is becoming."

> —Vicki Spandel and Ruth Culham,
> from training materials developed in 1993

Portfolios have the potential to be useful to teachers and students in two ways. First, portfolios can help us help our students to accomplish some of the harder goals we set for them—developing critical thinking and self-reflection skills; becoming aware of their own thinking; managing and evaluating their own learning. They can motivate students, help them discover who they are as learners, and boost their self-concept.

These reasons for doing portfolios are *instructional*; the process of doing the portfolio will itself promote desirable outcomes in student learning and motivation. However, not all portfolio activities are created equal, and not everything that is labeled a portfolio will promote the student skills listed above. The key is *student control*. Portfolios are a tool for learning and motivation to the extent that students determine what should go in the portfolio, why it should go in, what story the contents tell, and how they should be organized and displayed.

"By encouraging students to engage in self and peer evaluation, teachers empower students to take control of their own learning. When students help determine the criteria for assessment, they can make reasonable decisions about the quality of their own work. By engaging students in self-assessments, students learn they are ultimately responsible for their own learning. It is in this area that portfolios are so powerful."

> —Robert Tierney, *et al.*,
> "Portfolio Assessment in the Reading–
> Writing Classroom," page 59

The second way portfolios can be useful is that they are a good way to collect information about students in order to document what they know and are able to do. More and more districts and states are asking students to demonstrate their attainment of specific learning objectives (collaborative worker, good communicator, etc.) by building a case using a portfolio. Similarly, portfolios could be used to demonstrate to employers or colleges that one has the skills and attitudes necessary to be successful. These uses for portfolios are primarily *assessment* uses that enable us to determine an individual's level of skills and abilities.

Clearly, these uses are not mutually exclusive. For example, students can learn a lot about themselves and begin to take control of their learning during the process of assembling an employment portfolio. Likewise, promoting critical thinking by helping students apply criteria to their portfolio selections can result in a product that can be used for assessment.

Creating Portfolios for Success in School, Work, and Life provides a nice blend of instructional and assessment uses for portfolios, with the primary emphasis on instruction and student self-control. The exercises are designed to promote student self-reflection ("What am I good at?" "What do I like to do?") and critical thinking ("What would demonstrate these skills and interests to others?" "How can I present a believable case?"). The student book also helps students determine what an audience might want to see, consider various uses for portfolios, meet specific requirements for portfolios, and demonstrate employability skills.

Teachers who are most likely to find *Creating Portfolios* useful will probably be those who:

○ are willing to turn control over to students (can you trust your students to pick their best work?),

○ are willing to take risks (one never knows what students will come up with),

○ are flexible (students can go in many different directions),

○ value and emphasize thinking skills,

○ see themselves as coaches/mentors rather than dispensers of information, and

○ believe that students should take an active role in learning.

Portfolios can be a powerful tool for learning and assessment if we approach the task as a self-discovery experience for students. *Creating Portfolios* is a tool that can assist students in this process.

Judith A. Arter
Unit Manager, Evaluation and Assessment
Northwest Regional Educational Laboratory
Portland, Oregon

Introduction

I created my first portfolio almost twenty years ago, when I went in search of my first full-time teaching job. Because I was involved in writing and painting—fields in which people traditionally present themselves to editors and clients with a portfolio of their work—I assumed that presenting a teaching portfolio would be a logical way to convince administrators to hire me. In each interview, I could always count on the portfolio to get the attention of the interviewers.

In an era before desktop publishing, a simple white label on my portfolio cover announced:

> *Portfolio*
> Education and Arts
> Martin Kimeldorf

After completing a liberal arts degree with an emphasis on history and drama, I earned my first teaching certificate in Industrial Education. I hit upon the idea of presenting myself as a person who enjoyed integrating different disciplines. I wanted to suggest that technology or industrial arts could be integrated with the liberal arts. The table of contents in my first teaching portfolio listed some fifteen samples from my previous escapades in industrial arts, alternative education, and theater. Samples included:

- a listing of completed college and special course work,
- certificates I had received for presenting at conferences,
- articles and brochures printed about a program serving adjudicated youth in an after-school program which integrated the study of mini-bikes with the study of art,
- fliers for conferences I helped organize about youth at risk,
- letters confirming the selection of my plays for production, and
- a book of poetry which the adjudicated youth produced.

My portfolio portrayed me as a person who was comfortable participating in multiple disciplines. Later, when I earned a Master's Degree in Special Education, I added the following to my portfolio:

○ a brochure I wrote for recruiting peer tutors into my special education classes,

○ press releases and reviews about my handicap awareness play, which won several awards, and

○ more fliers from conferences at which I had presented.

As each job interview warmed up, I found the moment to introduce my portfolio. Typically, the principal didn't know what to do with it at first, so he or she just thumbed through it. This novel way of presenting my story—with words, pictures, and documents—led to some very interesting conversations.

Once I was asked how theater and industrial education could be integrated. This was a question I was dying to answer. I described a visionary school where the study of history or culture might be examined in a play production. While students in English analyzed and adapted the play, a group in wood shop would build a set that was designed in an art class and lit by science students studying electricity. It was only a fantasy twenty years ago, but it illustrated the kind of teacher I might be. As a result, I was one of the first graduates hired that spring.

My portfolio was also a useful screening device for both the principal and me. I was a job-seeker who presented myself as a bit different, using a slightly different communication tool. If the principal was receptive, that suggested a bright future for both of us. If not, I was off to another interview. In the end, I was hired by principals who understood what I was trying to do and welcomed my out-of-the-ordinary approach.

Recently I compiled a portfolio for my first art exhibit. I was able to enhance the product this time by using a computer. The gallery owner used the portfolio to decide which paintings to hang. The theme or title I had selected, "Flights of Color," was used in the subsequent advertising. On opening night, several guests thumbed through the portfolio in an effort to better understand the art and the artist.

Many teachers today are excited about the prospect of their students developing portfolios. A portfolio is an excellent vehicle for self-evaluation, reflection, communication, goal-setting, and inspiration. Thanks to computers and multimedia, the range of expression is almost limitless. One can create great covers and displays with clip art, scanned images, and printouts from charts, and even produce computer-coordinated presentations. Of course, one can still include "low-tech" items such as collages, actual objects, and letters of acknowledgment. Portfolios have so much potential in the classroom that it's no wonder teachers are enthusiastic about them.

To date, however, far more teachers have attended workshops on portfolios than have actually *created* portfolios. If this includes you, I strongly suggest that you spend a weekend reviewing your old clippings, report cards, photos, yearbooks, college papers, certificates, awards, and other historical doodads. Then assemble your mementos in a portfolio-type scrapbook. Do this *before* introducing portfolios to your students. You'll appreciate the complexity of the challenge and know firsthand the pleasure of producing the product. And when you show your class that you, too, have had the "portfolio experience," they will be more likely to follow you into the process.

Creating Portfolios for Success in School, Work, and Life flows out of my experience in producing portfolios, doing personal research on the topic, and writing other books for students and educators. I have tried to make the student book clear, accessible, and student-friendly, which should also make it teacher-friendly. I hope that it bridges the gap between enthusiastic theorists and the front-line reality of teaching all day. I hope that the exercises and examples make your job easier to the point where portfolio production becomes second nature for both you and your students. This Teacher's Guide adds some background and additional pointers that will help you lead your students through the process.

As you use *Creating Portfolios* in your classroom, you may find that you have a different experience or point of view. If so, I'd like to hear about it. I am also considering the possibility of collecting portfolio samples from across the country and compiling them into a portfolio scrapbook. If you have any comments, questions or suggestions, write to me at:

Free Spirit Publishing Inc.
217 Fifth Avenue North, Suite 200
Minneapolis, MN 55401-1299
help4kids@freespirit.com

I look forward to hearing from you. If you would like a reply, please include a stamped, self-addressed envelope.

Martin Kimeldorf
Tumwater, Washington

Creating Portfolios in Your Classroom

The Challenge

The subject of oneself is a most difficult writing topic. At first it may sound like fun, even interesting (we hope), but in reality the writing is based on one of the most elusive forms of knowledge: self-knowledge. This is why early lessons in *Creating Portfolios* are designed to help students think about their life experiences.

The difficulty of writing about oneself is summed up in the proverb, "We don't know who discovered water, but it probably wasn't a fish." Immersed in our own life waters, we rarely perceive what surrounds us, what creates us, and what we leave behind.

Producing a portfolio or résumé forces one to confront three critical life-planning questions:

- What have I accomplished?
- Who am I?
- What do I want to become?

Answering these questions is challenging, disturbing, and ultimately thrilling. Do you recall how you felt when you saw the final draft of your résumé coming out of the printer? You might have remarked, "That's me. I guess I have done a few things in my time!" For students, the final reward is looking into the mirror and seeing beyond the awkward adolescent to the emerging adult.

Jeremiah's Portfolio

Journals, scrapbooks, and portfolios hold the bits and pieces which sum up our lives. They give us a chance to look backwards, take stock of the moment, and dream of a future. A portfolio, at its best, is a visual story or autobiography. Therefore, the full potential of a portfolio is best described in the context of a story—in this case, the story of a student named Jeremiah, for whom creating and presenting a portfolio became a culminating event in his high-school education. It illustrates how a portfolio can not only record a life, but also help to define it.

Jeremiah never thought much about where high school would lead. His first year was tough—for him, high school was a world of rules, forms, faces, and changes. The portfolio-scrapbook assignment at the end of his freshman year was just another burden weighing him down. No one could adequately explain why he should do a portfolio. His freshman teachers dutifully lectured him about the importance of keeping track of one's learning; they explained that the scrapbook (a less formal portfolio) would help him develop the "portfolio habit" which would feed into the senior project required for graduation. When he presented his scrapbook to a review board, Jeremiah was a bit intimidated. He never really felt comfortable talking about himself in front of a group.

His senior year arrived sooner than he thought. Now it was time for his final portfolio. Jeremiah wasn't overly excited about the assignment. He still didn't understand the point of creating a portfolio. Besides, it looked like a lot of work; his teachers had said that it might take anywhere from 10 to 20 hours.

At the beginning of his senior year, his teachers suggested that he start collecting samples of his finest work—reports, essays, journals, assignments, awards, certificates. The problem was, Jeremiah couldn't think of anything to collect. There wasn't much he liked about school besides lunch and band practice.

He reluctantly began the self-assessment exercises in the workbook. Fortunately, the exercises encouraged students to include samples from experiences outside of school. Jeremiah found some old pictures from his sophomore year community service project, when he worked at a local bird refuge. Later, after the project was completed, he had continued to volunteer at the refuge, going on his own or with his Aunt Thelma. He hadn't minded giving up his weekends because he loved working outdoors clearing trails and streams. Once he and his aunt together had made a chart showing the many different birds that lived in the refuge.

Jeremiah couldn't include any awards or letters like some of the other students—he didn't have any. But one of the workbook exercises asked him to list the kinds of favors or help people often asked of him. This reminded him of the volunteer work he had contributed to Teen Hotline during his junior year. He found a brochure about the program. Another question asked him to describe a challenge he had met or an example of a time when he had been persistent. All he could think of were the endless music lessons his mom had driven him to after school on Tuesdays when he was in middle school. They finally paid off when he was selected for the band in his sophomore year of high school. He loved the trips and competitions, the discipline and the order of marching.

Now, as he constructed his final senior year portfolio, Jeremiah chose samples representing his work in the school band, his peer counseling experience with Teen Hotline, his gainful employment at a local restaurant (starting the summer before his senior year), and his volunteer experience at the bird refuge.

A picture of a worthy young man was emerging from the portfolio samples. Jeremiah sorted his photos, letters, and art work according to a system he had learned in the career education center. The system suggested that one's talents could be classified by the degree to which they involved working with three areas: Data, People, or Things (DPT). Jeremiah grouped his samples into three piles. He noted that many of them involved helping or serving people. This matched the results of his career and leisure interest tests. His advisor suggested that he include the printout from the career test in his portfolio. Jeremiah chose a final sequence that emphasized all the different ways in which he had worked with or for people or provided service to others.

He knew that the outline he used to organize his samples would be re-used later to prepare his oral presentation. In his freshman year, Jeremiah had been permitted to select three of the people who would serve on his review board. He had invited his special education teacher, his Aunt Thelma, and a graduating senior student. Now, in his senior year, he thought about the many people in his life who might be interested in hearing about his portfolio. He decided to invite his mother, his employer, and a counselor from the local community college who had helped him with his college application forms. He was already feeling better about the presentation. The outline gave him confidence and helped him to feel prepared.

There were many details that still needed attention. Jeremiah used the computer to scan images including a poster advertising the school band. He asked his employer for a letter of reference. He prepared a tape of his favorite band song to be used as background music during his oral presentation. He created a table of contents and wrote a final evaluation. He returned to the computer to finalize his caption, titles, and sample descriptions. Meanwhile, he consulted vocabulary lists to strengthen his descriptions.

When the hour for his oral presentation finally arrived, Jeremiah's slightly trembling hands reminded him of his first presentation four years ago. Halfway through the presentation, the community college counselor asked him to evaluate the different software he had used to scan his graphics. The band teacher walked by the room, heard the background music, and came inside to shake Jeremiah's hand. That meant a lot to Jeremiah. Then his mother told a story about a scared little freshman who had today become a man.

His employer asked him why he had chosen a psychology major for college. Jeremiah pointed to his portfolio. "My story is mostly about working with people," he explained. The employer nodded, and then suggested that he could also use his "people skills" to carve out a career in sales.

The moment for Jeremiah's dramatic ending was at hand. He looked up slowly, a slight smile wandering across his face. "I have chosen to evaluate my experience by responding to the portfolio evaluation question, 'What symbol and title would I put on my portfolio cover to tell the reader about the person inside?'"

Taking a deep breath, he continued, "I would use the title from a story I read in my Home and Family Life Personal Development class. It was called 'The Tale of the Persistent Dreamer.' Looking back over the past four years, I see that my portfolio reads like a map. It tells where I have been and where I might go next. Yes, it took me about 20 hours to get ready for today. And I think that many years from now, I'll enjoy turning the pages, thinking about how my story turned out."

Jeremiah's presentation took just 12 minutes, but it covered his entire school life. In that short time, he told a story which connected his past to a future he hoped to craft.

What a Portfolio Is—and Isn't

Creating Portfolios leads students to create a well-defined portfolio. My model is different from others that stress a particular educational purpose, such as alternative assessment, writing, or documentation for specific course objectives. In my model, a well-crafted portfolio becomes a vehicle for promoting three important skills: self-awareness, self-assessment, and communication. Students become more self-aware as they gather samples for possible inclusion in their portfolio. They practice self-assessment as they choose and sequence their samples. They communicate when they share their portfolio with others.

Webster's Collegiate Dictionary, Tenth Edition, defines "portfolio" as "a hinged cover or flexible case for carrying loose papers, pictures, or pamphlets...a set of pictures (as drawings or photographs) either bound in book form or loose in a folder." *The Random House Dictionary of the English Language,* unabridged, defines it as "a flat, portable case for carrying loose papers, drawings, etc." Neither definition—and, in fact, no traditional definition I was able to find—says anything about a portfolio serving as an alternative grading system.

Although portfolios can play a useful role in *supplementing* existing grading systems, common sense (and recent research) suggests that because they are so varied, they cannot easily be used as the *only* means of grading or comparing students. When they are, teachers are suddenly faced with the problems of time-consuming evaluation and awkward storage. To enable portfolios to be evaluated and graded, schools are forced to dictate precisely what goes into them. Students stop having a say about what samples to include in their portfolios, and the experience ceases being an expression of one's talents and becomes instead a simple folder collection of one's school work.

It is my opinion—and my experience both in the classroom and in my own life bears me out—that a portfolio is a reporting and communication tool. The student creating the portfolio should be allowed to decide what to report and communicate, with appropriate guidance from the teacher and other involved adults. A portfolio should be used to help a student gauge his or her own growth and accomplishment. When this happens, the portfolio becomes a means of celebration, and the portfolio presentation serves as a rite of passage, a special occasion for demonstrating and applauding the student's competence.

For more on the topic of portfolio assessment, see pages 19–20.

Adapting This Model for Your Students

Should a full-blown portfolio be required for all students regardless of age, grade, or ability level? In my opinion, the answer is no. I believe that the model presented in *Creating Portfolios,* if used in its entirety with no adaptation, is most appropriate for secondary and post-secondary students. If you are planning a school-wide or district-wide portfolio program for earlier grades, you will need to adjust this model or design your own. Following are some suggestions on how this model might be adapted for different levels. Use them as a springboard for your own ideas.

For tips on adapting these materials for students with special needs, see pages 35–39.

Elementary School

My model is not intended for students in elementary school. There are many other models better suited to this age group. For example, *Student Portfolios,* published by the National Education Association (see page 56), describes some useful approaches for very young students. However, if you wish to prepare your elementary students for creating portfolios in the upper grades, you can emphasize the simple collection and organization of materials for a scrapbook. To me, a scrapbook is the precursor to a portfolio.

Having your students gather samples in a shoe box, organize them chronologically, and create basic captions would help to establish the "portfolio habit." The final product will probably be similar to a family photo album. Students should include a table of contents at the beginning. Each item listed should have a basic bibliographic reference stating the title, source (where it came from), and date.

The portfolio presentation should be an informal show-and-tell or part of a parent-teacher-child conference. You might ask the parent(s) to make positive comments about the contents on a written form. Your form might include questions like the following:

❍ Which sample were you most impressed with?

❍ Did you learn something new about your child or his/her education?

❍ What is something you would like to see added to next year's portfolio assignment?

⚙ Would you be willing to serve on a portfolio review panel for other students next year?

For self-evaluation, I would ask the student to answer these basic questions:

⚙ Why is each sample important to you? Why did you include it?

⚙ Which sample is the most important to you personally? Why?

Middle School

Depending on your students and their capabilities, you may use *Creating Portfolios* as is or choose and adapt the exercises you think will work best. You may need to provide more structure for the sample selection process, and you may wish to suggest a scrapbook approach. Each item should have a bibliographic or cataloging reference (title and source, including when, where, and why).

The experience should include some form of oral presentation or small-group review, perhaps before a group of peers or older students from a nearby high school. For self-evaluation, I would ask the student to answer the following questions:

⚙ Why is each sample important to you? Why did you include it?

⚙ What does each sample demonstrate about you as a person? What talent or character trait does it illustrate?

⚙ Which sample is the most important to you personally? Why?

⚙ Which classes in high school might match your current interests and talents?

Early High School (Grades 9–10)

You might use the complete program in the student book or scale it down. As one option, you could have your students create a personal portfolio or "yearbook" of their first year in high school. As another option, you could have them demonstrate beginning research skills in an expert portfolio by choosing, then pursuing a topic in which they would like to become "expert."

Later High School and College (Grades 11 & up)

The soup-to-nuts approach is recommended at this stage. In other words, turn your students loose on the complete program described in the student book. You may want to have them present their portfolios to an audience of potential college placement personnel, employers, scholarship committees, etc. Or, if you prefer, you can ask students to create an expert or project portfolio tied to a particular project or class.

Also appropriate for this level is the employability portfolio described on pages 41–48.

Electronic Portfolios: A Cross-Grade Option

You may have noticed that a lot is being written about electronic portfolios. At this stage, it is not clear if these will simply become software databases—storage for pictures, sound, or words—or more complex multimedia documents. In my opinion, software that only holds information is no different from an empty shoe box or manila folder. The high-tech (or low-tech) holding device is not the critical element; it's the contents that matter. The success of a given portfolio reflects neither the shoe box nor the hypertext document, but rather the process employed in creating the portfolio itself.

Since I am recommending scrapbooks for elementary and middle school students, it might be worth examining a scrapbook project that is innovative both in its approach and in the media it employs: an online network.

The ScrapBook Writing Project, created by Emery Roth II at Shepaug School in Washington, Connecticut, has gained a national reputation for helping kids learn more about who they are and how they are similar to and different from other people around the country. This interdisciplinary, multicultural, cross-grade program uses computer telecommunications to link students in informal and formal writing. The culminating product is a scrapbook "chapter" of student writings, and the culminating celebration is an online "party" or chat session. Students share experiences in weekly informal postings on electronic bulletin boards. Eventually they share essays and poems describing themselves and their schools, as well as the people, places, treasures, and traditions of their communities.

ScrapBook entries describe dirt roads and street fairs, shopping malls and amusement parks, the view from the top of an apple tree and the quiet at the bottom of a closet, grits and latkes, gang wars, special grandmas, family bibles, a pet rat, and a special neighbor who sits all day on his front porch playing a harmonica.

An 11th grade social studies class in Lafayette, Georgia, described the things around them that reminded them of their Civil War past. An American Literature class at the southern end of the Berkshire Mountains wrote about the places near them that evoked the stories and landscapes of Nathaniel Hawthorne and Washington Irving. There are chapters of treasured recipes in which each recipe is followed by a description of its importance and the traditions it represents. The students at Vincent School in Milwaukee, Wisconsin, contributed a chapter called "FutureSchool."

ScrapBook chapters are exchanged between participating schools and added to an official online ScrapBook Library containing chapters from all over the country dating back to 1989.

This project engages people across all generations, from elementary school to senior citizens. What would it be like if we could share portfolio samples in a similar manner?

For more information, check out *The ScrapBook Curriculum ToolKit*; see page 56.

Getting Started

Deciding Who's Responsible

One of the most basic decisions you must make is the degree to which the student will be responsible for the overall portfolio design and selection of portfolio samples. Your decision will reflect how you define "portfolio" and the purpose you think a portfolio should serve.

CONTINUUM OF PORTFOLIO OPTIONS

Student-designed Student-selected	General guidelines Joint selection	Teacher or school prescribed
Purposes: Showcase/celebrate talents Self-evaluation	*Purposes:* Self-evaluation General evaluation	*Purposes:* Student or course evaluation

Audiences

Agencies, employers, customers	Students, colleges	School, family

○ At the far left of the continuum is the portfolio designed by the student, with the student having complete autonomy in creating the final product and deciding what it will include.

This kind of portfolio is well-suited to a culminating project or graduation requirement, where the student is asked to sum up his or her educational experiences and present the story in a portfolio format. It may be presented to community members and is primarily of benefit to the individual student.

○ At the far right of the continuum is the portfolio determined by the teacher or school.

Typically, the teacher gives students a list of required items based on course content. The overriding purpose here is student or course evaluation, and the products tend to possess a certain consistency or standardized quality. The primary consumers (audience) are the school and family.

○ At the center of the continuum is the portfolio that combines elements of both extremes.

The teacher or school may hand out general guidelines that require some specific items and leave the rest up to the student. Evaluation is de-emphasized and the primary purpose is one of showcasing the student's talents and/or celebrating his or her learning. These kinds of portfolios work well for interdisciplinary courses, culminating projects, and project portfolios.

The *Creating Portfolios* student book emphasizes the portfolios at the far left and center—student-designed and general guidelines. Exercise 2: Brainstorming about Student Portfolios (student book pages 14–17) provides support for those teachers who want to pursue a more prescriptive model.

I hope that *all* portfolios encourage students to bring in samples of work related to experiences outside of school. Regardless of which portfolio option you choose, I strongly recommend that you have your students complete Exercise 1: Brainstorming about Expert, Personal, and Project Portfolios (student book pages 10–13). This exercise will help them to visualize and appreciate the wide range and variety of samples which can be included in a portfolio. Even if you require very specific kinds of samples, students need to know the bigger picture. The portfolio skills they are learning in your class may be required later in a more general fashion for graduation, employment, and applications for grants or scholarships.

Identifying the Audience

Identifying the audience for your students' portfolios will help you to pinpoint the purpose. Are you asking students to produce a portfolio primarily for themselves, your course, their parents, community members, a local training school or college, people the student identifies as important, or some combination of these? Once you identify the audience, you can then decide what they will want and need to see, and this will suggest the criteria for a successful portfolio.

If you find that the audience is too broad, I suggest that you bring your focus back to the needs of the student. How will the portfolio help the student review his or her past experiences and thus serve as a guide for future work and learning? Exercise 6: Brainstorming about Your Audience (student book pages 36–38) gets students thinking about the people who will see their portfolio and how this affects the contents.

Storing Portfolios

Do your students' portfolios become part of their cumulative files, or should they be kept at home? Who should have access to them, and when? I suggest that a portfolio is a personal product which the student should retain possession of, and only relinquish briefly for evaluation and presentation purposes. This also eliminates for you the problems of storing and safeguarding 20–30 (or more) awkwardly shaped, sometimes fragile, and often irreplaceable sample collections. However, if you plan to give your students regularly scheduled class time to work on their portfolios, you probably will want to make some temporary storage arrangements—perhaps a closet shelf where students can stack their shoe boxes (or other devices used for storing samples).

Determining How Much Class Time to Spend on Portfolios

The more class time you can devote to demonstration, instruction, review, and guided practice for portfolios, the better the results will be. Following is one sample scenario for you to consider. It spreads portfolio preparation over a period of nine weeks, which is usually enough time for students to gather, sequence, and finalize acceptable portfolios. In this scenario, you should plan to spend about one to two class periods per week per portfolio assignment.

Weeks 1–2: Introduction to Portfolios and Self-Assessment

- Exercise 1: Brainstorming about Expert, Personal, and Project Portfolios
- Exercise 2: Brainstorming about Student Portfolios
- Exercise 3: What Could You Put in Your Shoe Box?

Weeks 3–6: Collecting and Organizing Samples

- Exercise 4: A Personal Inventory
- Exercise 5: Weekly Portfolio Log
- Exercise 6: Brainstorming about Your Audience
- Exercise 7: Selecting Your Samples
- Exercise 8: Analyzing Your Samples

Weeks 7–9: Preparing the Final Product

- Exercise 9: Outlining Your Portfolio
- Exercise 10: Writing Basic Descriptions
- Exercise 11: Enriching Your Descriptions
- Exercise 12: Finalizing Your Descriptions

Introducing Portfolios to Your Students

The best way to introduce the concept and experience of a portfolio to your students is to bring one in and show it to them. This could be a portfolio that you have made, or one that another student has made.

Show your students the title page (perhaps on an overhead projector). Ask them to guess what might be in the portfolio. Show them the table of contents and ask them to speculate on who the audience might be. Then show some or all of the samples, depending on the length and complexity of the portfolio.

Afterward, ask your students to guess how long it took to complete the portfolio (typically 10–20 hours). Ask if they can imagine what the author felt like when he or she finished the portfolio and shared it with an audience.

Tell your students that they will have the opportunity to make their own portfolios. Briefly explain some of the benefits of a portfolio, both personal and professional. You may want to read aloud the story of Jeremiah's Portfolio on pages 7–10 of this Teacher's Guide.

Assessment Issues

....

Educators are generally in agreement that portfolios are excellent tools for helping students assess their interests, talents, learning, and growth. But when portfolios are used as alternative methods for evaluating and comparing students or schools, a heated debate usually follows.

First, when entire states or districts elect to use portfolios for comparison purposes, a tremendous amount of time is required from assessment teams composed of staff and community members. Some teachers report having to spend an additional six hours each week managing and evaluating portfolios.

Second, the question invariably arises as to the reliability of grading portfolios. The more freedom students are given to select their samples, the more diverse their portfolio products are, and the harder it becomes to compare and evaluate these "apples and oranges." In fact, some studies suggest that the reliability of grading portfolios is very low unless teachers, administrators, or state agencies take steps to standardize the contents of the portfolios.

Some schools require that portfolios contain pre- and post-tests along with early and late samples of work to show student growth. Other programs require the inclusion of first and final drafts, specific software samples, certain types of math problems, etc. Unfortunately, these practices can eventually lead to standardization and subsequent teaching to the test standards—the very thing portfolios were not supposed to do. Soon the portfolio is looking less and less like the story of a student and more and more like the database of an administrator.

I am generally not in favor of grading portfolios except in the most general way. I am adamantly opposed to using them to compare schools or students or districts. But if you want or need to evaluate portfolios for class grading purposes, then it is important to develop a flexible and economical rubric. By "economical," I mean simple to follow and use, as opposed to detailed and lengthy with abstract criteria. The chart below may serve as a starting point.

This chart also appears in the student book as part of Exercise 6: Brainstorming about Your Audience (pages 36–38). The first two categories are filled in, and students are asked to complete the chart with criteria they think are important. If possible, you may want to incorporate some of your students' suggestions as you determine whether and how to evaluate their portfolios.

The very best feedback takes the form of a dialogue between student and evaluator(s). Suggestions for this kind of "education celebration" are found on pages 29–31 of this Teacher's Guide.

PORTFOLIO EVALUATION FORM

Demonstrates the following qualities	Experienced 3	Skilled 2	Entry Level 1
Completeness	10 or more samples	5–9 samples	1–4 samples
Neatness	Clean, easy to view	Somewhere in between	Messy or sloppy
Front matter	Cover, table of contents, introductory materials	Cover, table of contents, acknowledgments	Cover
Organization and design	Consistency in design elements Combines more than one organizational scheme	Follows a pattern (chronological, thematic talents, etc.) Uses dividers, labels, or descriptive material for samples	Fragmented or piecemeal design Follows a pattern for the most part
Back matter or self-evaluation	Evaluates self, includes goals, comments about issues larger than self	Evaluates self and sets goals for future	Evaluates the samples or the effort involved in creating the portfolio
Creativity	Samples and organization are unique	Contains several unique samples	Contains one unique sample
Content (when specific content or samples are prescribed. A specific rubric may be substituted for this category)	Goes beyond basic mastery to application Offers insights and demonstrates integration into other areas	Shows mastery of basic skills, vocabulary and concepts	Demonstrates basic or rudimentary skills Some gaps in skills

Evaluators should be familiar with the *Creating Portfolios* student book or with portfolios in general. If you know in advance how the portfolios will be evaluated—if you are given specific criteria ahead of time—then you should communicate these to your students and to other teachers as soon as possible, perhaps in one of your beginning lessons.

The Exercises

....

The following comments are intended to give you some additional background and insight into each exercise. You will also find ideas here for expanding on the student book lessons and content.

Exercise 1: Brainstorming about Expert, Personal, and Project Portfolios
(Student book pages 10–13)

Students are asked to consider these types of portfolios first, before the student portfolio. They are the most fun to think about, and the process of brainstorming about them gives students a broad overview of what a portfolio can be. These portfolios stir the imagination.

If you are having your class create student portfolios, you may want to incorporate aspects of project, expert, and personal portfolios into that project. For example, you might encourage your students to include a special section that demonstrates something they're expert in or feel deeply about.

Exercise 2: Brainstorming about Student Portfolios
(Student book pages 14–17)

This exercise offers you the opportunity to prescribe what needs to be included in your students' portfolios. If the portfolios will become a critical part of an assessment process, then the audience must be well defined in advance so students will include samples which meet the audience's expectations. The Specific List Worksheet on pages 16–17 of the student book gives you a quick and convenient way to check on your students' understanding of the portfolio assignment.

Exercise 3: What Could You Put in Your Shoe Box?

(Student book pages 20–22)

Just before students begin to consider collecting samples in earnest, they should once again broaden their range of possibilities. The shoe box is a refreshingly low-tech alternative in an increasingly high-tech world. Teacher Sharon Moorehead uses paper grocery bags with her students; other teachers have used plastic containers. Whatever method you choose, you will need to decide (as noted earlier) how to handle the storage. Will the students' shoe boxes and other portfolio materials be stored in your room, or will the students be responsible for them?

There are two ways you can assist your students in collecting items for their shoe boxes. First, whenever you hand back papers in class that might be included in a portfolio (essays with good grades and/or positive comments, tests with high or improved scores, notes or letters with positive comments from you to your students), be sure to add a note saying, "Please consider putting this in your portfolio." Second, consider handing out "Certificates of Recognition" on a regular basis. You can create these on a computer or purchase them at an office supplies store, along with gold seals and stamps. Certificates don't always have to be for the most outstanding work. You might use them to recognize improvement, effort, planning abilities (as opposed to final products), leadership, or willingness to help others. These can be very important for students who might not otherwise ever receive a certificate, plaque, or award.

For students who have a low self-concept or limited experiences from which to draw upon when creating their portfolios, it is important to allow greater-than-usual flexibility in choosing samples. For example, some students may never have played football on a school or park team, but they have followed one or more professional teams religiously. Let them include newspaper clippings about their favorite teams. Some students may never have taken a leadership role in a food drive, but they have contributed to one and thought a great deal about homelessness. Let them include articles about the food drive and the homeless, and perhaps an essay describing why these articles are important to them.

In other words, give *all* of your students a chance to exhibit their interests without requiring direct involvement or mastery of an interest area.

Exercise 4: A Personal Inventory

(Student book pages 23–29)

This exercise is essential if you give your students the freedom to select their finest work. By considering their personal character traits, talents, finest moments, affiliations and memberships, challenges, and interests, they begin identifying samples they might include in their portfolios. This exercise is especially useful if you are asking your students to create portfolios as part of a graduation or culminating experience, or if you want the project to assist them in career development and self-assessment.

If you are using a prescriptive portfolio model, where students are required to include specific items, you may want to skip this exercise. On the other hand, both you and your students might learn something interesting from it.

Exercise 5: The Weekly Portfolio Log
(Student book pages 30–34)

This may be one of the most important exercises in *Creating Portfolios.* Note that the Portfolio Log form on pages 32–34 of the student book is reproducible, meaning that you may make multiple copies for classroom use. Students should complete a new Portfolio Log each week. Every so often—perhaps every two to three weeks—ask your students to bring their shoe boxes to class and share the contents (or, if you are storing them in the classroom, schedule a regular time for sharing samples). They will enjoy the feedback, and students who are having trouble coming up with samples may get ideas that will help them to add to their own portfolios.

For many students, one of the biggest challenges of creating a portfolio is staying on track with the sample collection process. The due date arrives all too soon, and they find themselves with only a few samples or samples that are poorly selected and disorganized. You may want to use the Portfolio Log as an incentive by announcing that students who turn them in weekly will earn points toward their final grade. Even if the final product falls short, they will have accumulated enough points for a passing grade. I also recommend this approach for students with special needs, since it gives them the chance to demonstrate archival skills and be evaluated on a periodic basis rather than waiting for an all-or-nothing evaluation on a final product.

Exercise 6: Brainstorming about Your Audience
(Student book pages 36–38)

Naturally you will need to identify the audience before assigning this exercise. Decide whether you want to invite "outsiders" (parents, neighbors, community members, employers), display finished portfolios in the library, have your students present them before a panel of experts, let students invite their own audience members, and so on.

You may want to have your students share their thoughts on who they would invite and what they think their audience members might expect to see. Tabulate the results to see if there is a consensus about expectations. This process will help students develop a sense of pride in what they are doing and a better understanding of the criteria they are expected to meet.

Exercise 7: Selecting Your Samples
(Student book page 39)

This exercise, combined with the weekly Portfolio Log, should give you a good idea of how individual students are progressing with their portfolios. You may want to schedule conferences so students can talk with you one-on-one about their lists. This exercise should fall at about the halfway point in the portfolio process, so students who are in trouble still have time to catch up.

Exercise 8: Analyzing Your Samples
(Student book pages 40–42)

This exercise asks students to analyze their samples with a coding system developed by the United States Department of Labor. This is not as complicated as it sounds, and the student book explains it clearly. A chart on student book page 41 gives students practice in using the coding system before applying it to their own samples. The following answers are recommended, but they are not hard-and-fast. You may want to consult with a career counselor for additional information and insights. Better yet, take your students on a field trip to a local career center or library and ask them to look up various jobs in the *Dictionary of Occupational Titles* (DOT) or computer databases.

In any event, what's important here is not that your students give "correct" answers. Rather, you want to make sure that they are beginning to understand how to classify experiences by the types of skills used.

WHAT'S THE SCORE?

Job	Data	People	Things
Tailor		X	X
Flower arranger		X	X
Miner		X	X
Ice cream truck driver		X	X
Teacher	X	X	?
Biologist	X		X
Animal trainer		X	X
Farmer		X	X
Counselor	X	X	
Secretary	X	X	
Cashier	X	X	
Lifeguard		X	X (Body)

Exercise 9: Outlining Your Portfolio

(Student book pages 45–50)

This exercise invites students to consider four possible ways of sequencing their samples: chronologically, by talents, thematically, and a combination of chronological and thematic. You may want to ask if anyone has another idea for sequencing portfolio samples.

To help your students grasp the general principal of organizing materials, and the more abstract concept of organizing them by themes, lead them through the following introductory exercise.

1. Begin by explaining that organizing a portfolio is like organizing a book. Say that a portfolio is like a specific type of book—an autobiography. Mention that book titles and covers are very important in book sales; a catchy title and attractive cover can make the difference between success and failure. Tell your students that a title must convey the book's message clearly and quickly, and that titles are sometimes supported by subtitles. Explain that a table of contents helps the reader see at a glance what the book contains.

2. Instruct your students to take out a blank piece of 8 1/2" x 11" paper. Say, "At the bottom, in the center, write 'The True Life Story of...,' then add your name. This is your subtitle. At the top, write a brief title—one to five words—that summarizes your life. In the space between your title and subtitle, add a drawing. Or write a description of a drawing you would like to see there—as if you're giving instructions to a graphic designer at a publishing house."

   If students need help getting started, invite them to brainstorm some possible titles for autobiographies. Write sample titles on the board. Encourage quick, intuitive thinking. If necessary, quickly review the rules of brainstorming: There are no "right" or "wrong" responses, and criticism isn't allowed.

3. After your students have written their titles, ask for volunteers to share what they wrote. Add their titles to the board. Then talk briefly about how, in a book, the table of contents supports the title. Invite students to brainstorm possible chapter headings for several of the sample titles listed on the board. Write their ideas beneath the titles.

4. Next, improvise a "review" of each "book." You might comment on the book title, how the story progresses (as indicated by the chapter titles), fascinating tidbits you "learned" about the author from reading the autobiography, and more. Keep it light and humorous—all in fun. You might do one or two of the reviews, then ask student volunteers to do the rest.

5. Finally, point out that a book title is like a main theme. The chapter titles in the table of contents are supporting themes. Explain that in a portfolio, the table of contents shows how the samples are organized. Later, it can be used for the oral presentation.

One teacher enriched this lesson by bringing in samples from his wife's employment portfolio. He told his students the kinds of career changes she was going through and showed them the samples she had collected. Then he had the students evaluate each sample, asking questions like, "Do you think she should include this sample? Why or why not? Would her audience—a prospective employer—be impressed by it?" Next, he asked the students to suggest ways to group or organize the samples.

The introductory exercise—with or without enrichment—is not only a good way to lead into Exercise 9. It also demonstrates the value of sharing ideas with others before deciding on a final format or outline for a portfolio.

As your students work through Exercise 9, be available to review the steps involved in outlining and to assist individual students in deciding which type of outline to use. Be sure to look carefully at the rough draft outlines; serious problems should be evident here and can be addressed before students create their final outlines.

Exercise 10: Writing Basic Descriptions

(Student book pages 53–55)

This exercise leads students through the process of adding titles and descriptions to their samples. Examples are provided, but you also may want to invite volunteers to share some of their titles and descriptions with the class. Have multiple copies available of the Sample Description Worksheet on page 55 of the student book.

Exercise 11: Enriching Your Descriptions

(Student book pages 56–58)

This exercise encourages students to go "beyond the basics" and add energy, detail, and a measure of sophistication to their sample descriptions. This is also good preparation for résumé writing. This enrichment activity can be made optional. Whether you use it will depend on a number of factors: your students' abilities, the time available, the types of portfolios your students are doing, the audience, and so on.

Word lists are provided on pages 77–79 of the student book.

Exercise 12: Finalizing Your Descriptions

(Student book pages 59–60)

You may want to have samples available of the options described on student book page 60, "Note." This exercise is another opportunity for students to share ideas and get feedback from others.

Finishing Touches

Pages 61–68 of the student book guide students through the process of adding the "finishing touches" to their portfolios. They choose a format, decide whether to add page numbers, create a cover and table of contents, write an introduction or Highlights Summary, and add back matter, which may or may not include a concluding self-evaluation statement.

It must be emphasized that the use of a portfolio for self-evaluation is a contribution by educators to the field of portfolio production. Therefore, to paraphrase from the "Note" on page 66, a concluding self-evaluation statement *only* belongs in a student or school portfolio. It *does not* belong in a portfolio that will be presented (now or later) to an employer, funding agency, or customer.

As an alternative to having students write concluding self-evaluation statements, you may use the questions on pages 66–68 of the student book to interview students about their portfolio experiences, individually or as a class exercise. Or hold an in-class panel discussion. Ask for volunteers to serve as panel members, then use the questions in the student book to direct the discussion.

On pages 49–54 of this Teacher's Guide, you'll find an enrichment exercise you may want to use at this time. If some students have already completed their portfolios, this exercise will encourage them to develop their skills further. A talents poster also makes an interesting cover for a portfolio.

The Portfolio Presentation

I cannot emphasize strongly enough that the portfolio presentation should be an *enjoyable* experience, not a stressful and anxiety-producing "final exam." If portfolios are to be graded, the grading should be done before the portfolios are presented to an audience. This way, students won't be worrying about their grades as they prepare for their presentations.

You may want to schedule practice sessions before the actual presentations. Encourage student "audience members" to pay close attention to each presentation and come up with at least one question to ask at the end. Have students rate each presenter's performance. On page 30, you'll find a rating form to copy and use.

In the *KIB Writes/KIB Speaks/KIB Reports* series (see page 57), I present various exercises designed to build confidence in public speaking. In those books, you'll find activities to help students develop effective voice qualities (volume, articulation, gesture, and modulation) and examples of how to prepare interesting speeches (ways to introduce and capture attention, the use of examples and details, how to summarize or conclude a speech).

When I invite people to a portfolio presentation—other teachers, parents, community members, and so on—I always send a personal letter to each audience member, explaining the process and their role in it. This helps everyone to know in advance what to expect and what will be expected of them. They tend to get more involved in the presentation and to ask better questions of the student presenters. On page 31, you'll find a sample letter inviting people to an end-of-the-school-year education celebration—a portfolio review.

PORTFOLIO PRESENTATION RATING FORM

Presenter's Name: _____ **Date:** _____

Evaluator's Name: _____

	Excellent		Average		Needs work
Has good posture 5	4	3	2	1
Smiles...5	4	3	2	1
Makes eye contact...5	4	3	2	1
Speaks in a clear and loud voice 5	4	3	2	1
Purposefully integrates samples from the portfolio into the presentation 5	4	3	2	1
Seems relaxed and comfortable 5	4	3	2	1
Uses some gestures and voice variety...................5	4	3	2	1
Emphasizes talents and accomplishments.............5	4	3	2	1
Presentation is well-organized 5	4	3	2	1
Answers questions with specifics or examples.......5	4	3	2	1
Demonstrates critical thinking, learning, reflection (uses phrases like "I never realized before...," "I learned...," "I have decided...," "As a result, I plan to...") 5	4	3	2	1

This is what I liked best about the presentation: _____

_____

_____

_____

Overall rating: I'd give this person a 5   4   3   2   1

Dear _____,

On May 26, the students in my Senior Class Project class will be asked to reflect on their year's experience in the class and share samples of their finest moments and greatest achievements. These samples will be included in student portfolios and presented to a Portfolio Review Board of parents, teachers, students, and community members. I am writing to invite you to be part of the Portfolio Review Board.

Over the past several weeks, my students have been collecting, selecting, and organizing samples that they feel represent their performance in the Senior Class Project class. Their samples might include any of the following:

* Examples of times when they took a positive risk

* Items demonstrating their accomplishments

* Teacher comments or assessments identifying their strengths or praising their progress

* Essays, journal pages, poems, etc. that show creative and original thinking

* Other expressions of creativity (art, video, audio, photographs, multimedia, etc.)

* Charts, graphs, posters, or overheads that display their best work

* Awards and other forms of recognition

I welcome your participation in this process of reflection, communication, and review. The portfolios have already been graded, so I will not be asking you to rate or evaluate the students' work. Rather, your role is one of observation, inquiry, commentary, and recognition.

For example, suppose that a student reads a short scene from a play he or she has written. As you listen and observe, you jot down a few notes on the skills the student might have used to write the play—setting the scene, creating interesting characters, writing believable dialogue. Following the portfolio presentation, you ask questions meant to help the student communicate about the experience in greater detail: "What inspired you to write your play?" "Are any of the characters based on real people in your life?" "How did you learn about...?" "How long did it take you to write your play?" Finally, you might end with an affirmation or two: "Writing a play is hard work. Congratulations on your persistence." "I noticed that one of your characters was able to speak up for himself, even when he was afraid of what might happen. That's a good example for anyone who sees your play in the future." "When you were reading your scene, I could actually see it in my mind. I wish I could hear the whole play!" Or you might conclude by focusing on the future: "Will you write more plays?" "Do you think you'd like to have a play produced?" "Would you like to direct a theater someday?"

The students and I look forward to this being a joyous event. I plan to hand out awards, certificates, and various other forms of recognition during the review. Please join us in our efforts to encourage community involvement in our school's learning experience.

Yours sincerely,

_____.

RESOURCES

RESOURCES

Portfolios for Special Learners

....

Sharon Moorehead's Tip Sheet for Adapting the Instruction and Materials

Sharon Moorehead is a teacher in Lacey, Washington

I have been teaching in the public school system for thirteen years in various subjects and grades including Special Education and regular education, kindergarten through high school. I have never found any one teaching method that works all the time, so I am always experimenting and trying alternatives. I'd like to share with you some modifications I made to Martin Kimeldorf's book, *Creating Portfolios for Success in School, Work, and Life.* Although these changes were made to make the program more accessible to students with special needs, Martin has told me, "Most of your suggestions apply to just about any learner."

I have worked with portfolios for four years, with the majority of that experience centered in a regular fifth-grade classroom. My students used portfolios to organize and reflect upon their work in the areas of math and language. As you no doubt will find out, the initial tasks of collecting and evaluating samples are often daunting and take a lot of time. But you are in for a surprise at the end of the year, when you see excited heads bobbing up and down, scanning portfolios, looking at each others' products, and bantering about the contents. I guarantee that this can happen, even in high school! It is for this reason that I love using portfolios to help my students highlight their unique qualities. This is especially important for students with special needs, for whom the typical school day contains few "highlighting" moments. Perhaps this is why I chose to pursue my dream at our district's new and innovative River Ridge High School. The administration here is committed to giving this special portfolio experience to all students.

As I started to work with high school students in 1993, I was surprised at how little confidence they had in their academic abilities. This perception doubled my interest in providing them with an experience where they could gain an understanding and confidence about themselves. At the end of my first high school cycle of portfolio creation, I can now report that my hopes were fulfilled, but not without some anxiety and risk-taking.

Originally the students approached the portfolio project with an uncertain attitude, but by the end they had "bought into" the importance of collecting or archiving samples and organizing them for display. Along with this, the students discovered that they had something worth showing, and their lives had special moments worth honoring. The following tips and adaptations helped us to reach this important stage.

General Tips

My best general advice is be to patient and spice your lessons with celebrations as students reach certain benchmarks in the creation of their portfolios: collecting ten samples, organizing their samples, or making a final oral presentation.

I recommend that you preview each lesson with the class. Sometimes this means beginning with a discussion which introduces new terms like "portfolio" or "reflection." Make this introduction as concrete and visual as possible.

I often try to use real products to spur interest. For instance, we once had an artist come in and show his portfolio. Before he opened the binder, he asked, "Can you guess what I have in here?" Another time, I brought in a photo album to start a discussion about reflection.

If our class discussion covers the essential points of a particular lesson, I skip reading the text material out loud and go right to the assignment. Sometimes I preview a worksheet page by displaying it on the overhead and doing the first half together with my students for practice. At other times, we brainstorm as a group lists of ideas which could apply to a given assignment before the students begin the work. The lists we generate provide students with correctly spelled "starter ideas" which can be easily adapted or re-used by individual students.

Another important process involves debriefing or reviewing and acknowledging effort. In my class, this often takes the form of asking students to share out loud what they have written or created. I set aside time for small-group discussions when the workbook pages are finished. The groups usually have from four to five students. I have found that some students build off the ideas of others, and this gives them confidence in their own ideas.

Collecting and Cataloging Samples

We start by examining our leisure interests or hobbies. This later evolves into discussions of other important life experiences. Many of the students are not always able at first to articulate why a given sample is important to them. As a result, I ask them do some simple reflective thinking and writing exercises. Students are asked to catalog their samples with statements that answer the following three questions:

1. What is the item you have brought to class? Give it a title or name.

2. Why is it important?

3. What does it say about you?

Some students get stuck on the second question. My solution is to engage them in a discussion which leads to an analysis of what the sample symbolizes in their life. I try to get them to dissect the effort that lay behind the artifact. A typical discussion might go something like this:

Teacher: "Weren't you on the football team?"

Student: "Yeah."

Teacher: "What did it take to be on the team? How much time did you have to spend at practice?"

Student: "We had to practice two hours every day and four hours for the game each week."

Teacher: "How long is the football season?"

Student: "About eight to ten weeks."

Teacher: "So that would mean at least ten hours of practice every week for at least eight weeks. How many hours of practice would you put in?"

Student: "That would be 80 hours."

Teacher: "Eighty hours sounds like a lot of time you put in to be on a football team. Wouldn't you be impressed by a team member who set a goal and worked hard to get there?"

A little adult coaching goes a long way, and before long the students can take on the responsibility. I often call on students to play the role of examiner. I ask, "Who'd like to ask the next question?" By the end of the lesson, kids are raising their hands, eager to ask questions. Being part of the process gets them caught up in creative thinking—just what I want!

I also hope that my students will develop a sense of the change or growth in their lives. This is particularly important when you consider the changes that future workers will have to go through. Currently, many experts believe that future workers will have to change careers (not just jobs) from five to seven times during their working lives. They will need to learn how to evaluate their skills and talents so they can constantly repackage them to match new opportunities as old jobs disappear or change.

Motivating Students to Bring In Enough Samples

Asking my students to bring in ten items by a particular date is asking for disappointment. Instead, I ask them to bring in three samples each week. I even make phone calls home to encourage the collection process. If students bring in items that are "valuable," like baseball cards, keys, trophies, etc., we take pictures or reproduce them on copy machines so the originals will not be damaged or lost. We then review what the students have brought in. Some students get ideas from seeing the samples of others.

All of this effort seems to pay off as we approach the third week, when a total of ten samples are due from everyone who wants to participate in our pizza party celebration. The pizza party provides the final "excuse" or motivation for some students. The party atmosphere gives us all some time to let down our official roles and engage in lively social conversation while playing various board games. Trust must be established with these students, if they are going to take the risk of sharing something that is important to them.

I have to admit that there have been times when I have been discouraged. I've had to constantly remind myself of the final goal or vision: students understanding and honoring their strengths and abilities. I want my students to be proud of their accomplishments and know that they will have more in their future.

Using Hands-On Alternatives to Outlining and Other Academic Tasks

When it comes time to outline the portfolios (Exercise 9 in the student book) and group the samples, we usually begin with an introductory exercise (see pages 25–26 of this Teacher's Guide). I discuss with my students how one goes about organizing collections of cards or compact discs. I ask them to draw a picture of a mock book which represents the story of their lives. Then I ask them to come up with a title and table of contents for their fictional autobiography. Finally, I "review" each book. I might praise the "fabulous story I just read about snowboarding and the gripping tale of getting lost in the woods." This is all done tongue-in-cheek and helps students prepare to organize the story of their own life.

For Exercise 9, I bring in binders and three-hole-punched plastic envelopes (sometimes called "sheet protectors"). I sell them to the students at cost and ask them to put their samples inside the envelopes (instead of mounting them on pages). Then I ask them to group their samples by what they have in common. I usually have to help a few students see the connections between some of their samples before they are able to come up with a theme for each group. Finally, we make up names for the groups, a process similar to creating a title and table of contents for a book. We record the names, and they become the outline sections. The outline is re-used as the table of contents.

In other words, students create their outlines by manipulating the samples. I call this "hands-on outlining."

Simplifying to the Core Task

When I first started using portfolios with my students, and it came time for them to write their introductions and conclusions, I asked myself, "How can I simplify this assignment to the essential skills? What is the core task?" I worked with Martin Kimeldorf to turn his sample outline for an introduction into a worksheet, and then we shortened the list of reflective questions to come up with the following five concluding questions:

1. Tell what you did to make a portfolio.

2. What is something you seem to be consistently good at, as demonstrated in your portfolio?

3. What parts of your portfolio reflect your career choice?

4. Which samples are your best or favorite pieces? Tell why they are effective or important.

5. What would grade would you give yourself for this portfolio? Justify your grade.

Employability Portfolio Models

An employability portfolio is designed to communicate a student's general career direction and accomplishments. The audience might include employers, vocational certification or review boards, vocational training program personnel, community advisory groups, or representatives from institutions where the student might pursue advanced training. This type of specialized portfolio summarizes a student's vocational training, work experience, and any other talents related to one's career. The samples to be included are typically drawn from job search materials, vocational classes, internships, apprenticeships, or cooperative work experience programs.

The employability portfolio can be further refined and shortened into a job search portfolio, which is then used as a tool for marketing one's employability in the labor market. In simplest terms, the highly focused job search portfolio operates like a visual résumé. In the not-too-distant future, it may play a useful role in the "virtual labor market" just emerging in the online world and providing electronic résumé databases, online job support and counseling services, and computerized employment research tools.

Employability Portfolio Overview

What might the general employability portfolio look like? There are many ways to approach this question. One model suggested by California's *Career-Technical Assessment Project (C-TAP) Portfolio Guidebooks* (see page 55) recommends creating a portfolio which includes work samples, letters of reference, samples of occupational research, and samples which demonstrate mastery of specified performance standards (learning outcomes) for vocational classes. Another model, developed by the Michigan State Board of Education and described in *Portfolio Information Guide, Employability Skills* (see page 55), asks students to use a "legal argument" format to prove or demonstrate employability across three domains: academic (which includes communications, mathematics, science, technology, and problem-solving skills), personal management skills (demonstrating responsibility, organization, flexibility, and career development), and teamwork skills (including compromising, leadership, and contributing).

Obviously there are many ways to build an employability portfolio. On page 43, you'll find a chart describing general categories of employability, corresponding subgroups, and typical work samples for each group. As you advise students about creating employability portfolios, you'll have to decide which specific categories and samples best reflect your local labor market conditions. You may want to seek input from local employment experts—counselors, employers, job search trainers, agencies, large and small businesses. Try to keep things simple and recognize that the hiring process is often driven by common sense and the fear of making the wrong decision. Avoid prescribing guidelines based on an analysis of the "global economy." Keep the focus on your local conditions. Remember that portfolios are not about *work*, they are about the individual *worker*. This means that the portfolio should reflect the individual. A portfolio—or a résumé— is most believable and convincing when it is rooted in the details of the individual's experience in the community, not in the jargon of job descriptions.

General Category	Subgroup	Examples of Portfolio Samples
General employability	Demonstration of career decision making efforts	• job interest or aptitude test • "job report" based on researching jobs both in the library and in person (the latter is called an informational interview) • journal entries about job shadowing • applications to training programs (apprenticeships, programs funded by the Job Training Partnership Act, Job Corps, vocational-technical schools) or higher education institutions (local community and four-year colleges) • goal-setting documents
	Evidence of completing successful work experiences	• attendance records • employer evaluations • letters of reference about work experiences • weekly journals or reports about the job experience • reports of hours and wages • committee participation
Technical proficiency, technical literacy	Performance indicators related to producing specific products, following procedures, or attaining mastery in a given field	• reading plans (blueprints or schematics) • organization charts • budgets or financial plans • certificates demonstrating mastery or granted by examination • specific documents from a field of study (medical chart, marketing brochure, underwater weld sample, financial statement, software output, emergency equipment, CPR card, safety test, customer satisfaction plan, database designed by the student, safety inspection sheet, marketing plan, pictures of a livestock competition, results from surveys, a public service announcement)
	Samples of technical proficiency (including photos, videos, computer displays, and actual artifacts from the workplace, vocational classes, or projects)	• lists of competencies mastered • charts showing hours or time completed in various areas of study • awards • certificates or licenses • vocational evaluations or aptitude tests
People and team skills	Evidence of leadership and cooperation skills	• participation in vocational competitions • membership in vocational or service clubs • completion of individual project or course of study • completion of group project • community service
	Communication and information-gathering skills related to world of work	• written, oral, nonverbal, listening skills • problem-solving, research, reporting
Job search survival skills	Documentation of mastering traditional job seeking methods and plans for job seeking	• résumés (paper) • flawless applications • letters of reference
	Documentation of mastering creative or self-directed job-seeking methods	• evidence of knowledge about various employment services (government, private, online services) • list of 15 potential network people • scripts or approaches to be used when networking • yellow pages summary of local businesses representing one's field of interest • electronic résumés • evidence of self-directed, active job seeking (contact forms for networking and phoning, time charts, etc.) • job interview practice rating forms, • daily/weekly job search planner

Job Search Portfolio Pointers

A job search portfolio is designed to demonstrate a student's job readiness for employers. The process of summarizing one's vocational preparation and experience will help the future job seeker prepare for interviews and résumé writing. Given that the average résumé is read for ten to fifteen seconds, it's essential to prepare a finely honed and targeted portfolio if this marketing tool is to get the employer's attention.

The length of the portfolio will depend on the situation. In the first instance, the job seeker leaves the portfolio with a virtual stranger, just as one would leave a résumé or application. If one hopes to capture the attention of a stranger, then the portfolio must contain extremely tight and concise text, surrounded by a generous amount of white space and supporting graphics. The portfolio in this scenario could be from two to four pages long. It is best left in person or introduced into a job interview.

The second situation is when the employer knows the job seeker or has previously expressed an interest in the individual. In this case, the job seeker can bring in a longer portfolio containing more examples.

Overall, the best approach is to develop a "working" portfolio, collecting samples of work in a general employability portfolio that may then be used to compile a short job search portfolio.

Sample Table of Contents for a Job Search Portfolio

This portfolio should emphasize the mastery of skills which relate to the specific occupation being sought. If possible, it should include something directly related to the place where one wants to work. For example, if the student wants to work in a restaurant, he or she should include any food handling certificates or health cards which may be required of all employees in food service by local or state agencies.

The job search portfolio should be designed to be quickly and easily read. While many of us could probably come up with a portfolio of ten pages or longer, I strongly recommend a shorter one—approximately four pages at the most. It should be printed back-to-back to make it appear as short as possible. Better yet, all four pages could be printed on both sides of a single sheet of 11" x 17" paper, as shown on the next page.

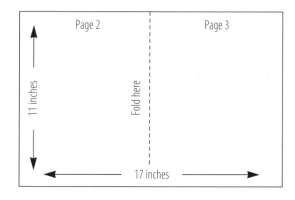

The front page or cover should include essential information similar to the heading of a résumé. Also like a résumé, it should include vital information: name, address, and message phone. In addition, it is helpful to include a job goal or brief description of the portfolio, as shown below. The cover should also include an inviting picture or graphic element, perhaps followed by a listing of the portfolio highlights.

**MARTIN KIMELDORF
TEACHING PORTFOLIO**

6705 Gold St., Corvallis, OR
Phone 555-7869, Message Phone 555-9988

[Picture of the job seeker teaching,
a thank you letter from a student,
an award, or other example of excellence]

- ✪ Creative lessons
- ✪ Emphasis on community connections
- ✪ Team player

Somewhere in the first few pages of the portfolio should be an introductory paragraph combined with a sample or visual element. The introduction could include a summary of career interests or goals and an encapsulated view of the achievements demonstrated in the portfolio. Goals should be realistic and should reflect present levels of experience and training. Both long-term goals and immediate goals should be covered. For example, a long-term goal of business management could be supported by a short-term goal of working in sales or marketing.

A table of contents may not be necessary in a short portfolio. If a table of contents is included, it should be limited to no more than one-half page of text. In some cases, much of this information can be included on the cover, as long as it doesn't crowd this critical first page.

The remainder of the portfolio should include three to five samples of work and experience. The samples can be captured in graphics, pictures, or photocopies—never the original items. With today's high-quality copy machines, original items are never needed except as master copies.

Each sample should be accompanied by a title and a brief summary of the skills it represents. Leaving lots of white space around each sample helps to dramatize it. Samples can be presented individually—one per page—or in a montage of visuals supported by captions.

Here are some examples of what could be included:

- An employer evaluation or letter of reference

- A job description listing one's duties and responsibilities.

- Any indicators of one's quality of work, achievement, or promote-ability. Examples:

  - being given increased hours

  - being given increased responsibility (training or supervising others, more job duties)

  - pay raises

  - attendance record at work

  - being given improved or expanded job titles

  - receiving employee recognition awards, privileges, rewards

  - demonstrating quality by a low error rate (never having to redo something, few rejects, few returns, etc.)

  - receiving compliments from typical customers or requests for one's personal service

  - helping to increase production, making procedures or services more efficient

  - any attempts to increase business in terms of customers, income, sales, and/or requests

○ Additional training achieved outside of traditional channels (work-shops, conferences, self-study programs, computer study, etc.). These can be indicated by a list, sample certificates, or name cards. A conference brochure lends credibility.

○ A list of any special projects one worked on or was responsible for. Examples: anything demonstrating how one improved procedures or productivity at work, such as a revised reporting procedure or organization chart for a tool room; a flier or brochure developed for a conference; a description of a community service project involving job-site employees; a list of any committees or organizations with which one was or is affiliated.

○ Evidence of having learned skills related to the position being sought. This might include lists of skills mastered and projects completed; recognition received from instructors; extra responsibilities assumed; leadership roles performed; clubs joined; grades earned; etc. Examples: developing menus for a day-care program; setting up safety rules or passing a rigorous safety test; videotaping a fundraiser; creating a newsletter; mastering a software program; researching a special problem; interviewing people; developing plans for a project; designing something; etc.

○ One or two letters of recommendation from employers (preferred), teachers, or other authority figures or people who play a special role in one's life (religious leaders, counselors, administrators, coaches, trainers, volunteer coordinators, etc.).

○ A printed résumé, as long as it is targeted at the specific employer or business and can be placed with the employer separately.

Emphasizing a Quality Job Search Education

In these competitive times, schools must play a more dynamic role in preparing students to successfully enter and navigate in the labor market. Increasingly, schools must emphasize "effective" job search techniques rather than the traditional ones. In other words, because a portfolio tends to be a printed product, we have often erred on the side of promoting the inclusion of the more conservative (and easy-to-include) job search documents—résumés, job descriptions, job applications. However, we must begin to ask students to include samples demonstrating self-directed and effective job search behaviors, including (among others) networking, cold-calling, persistent follow-up, and using a variety of approaches.

Consider asking students to include documentation using traditional techniques (applications, paper résumés, letters of reference) as well as samples of creative or effective job seeking—a list of networking prospects, addresses or resources for online résumé data banks, role-playing scripts for telemarketing and cold-calling, and questions used in occupational in-person research or informational interviewing.

Above all, don't just make these assignments without proper in-depth training. (For example, nothing is worse than asking students to bring back a letter of reference and then never telling them the protocols and methods which increase the odds of their receiving a good letter.) There are many excellent references you can turn to. The first resource you should be familiar with is Richard Bolles' *What Color Is Your Parachute?* (see page 56). This perennial bestseller will give you the widest possible view of career development and job seeking. In fact, readings or research from this work should be part of every employability portfolio.

Also, I have developed books you may find useful. *Job Search Education* contains sample network lists, phone call scripts, and sequences for acquiring letters of reference, among other helpful resources and tools. *Write Into a Job* is a workbook on how to produce a quality résumé. For information about these titles, see pages 57 and 56.

Two new "must-review" books include *Electronic Job Search Revolution* and *Electronic Résumé Revolution* by Joyce Kennedy and Thomas J. Morrow. See page 55.

It is amazing that even in today's increasingly volatile labor market, where people change jobs like hopscotchers, we have not yet institutionalized job search training. Only one in two hundred people gets a quality job search education. Perhaps this type of portfolio will better prepare students for survival in a world where they will constantly change jobs, and where each student's basic education includes an emphasis on job search education.

Talents Poster Exercise

You can get closer to your goals and dreams by using a daily exercise based on a Talents Poster. You'll start by making a poster about a talent you hope to use someday in the future. By staring at the poster and picturing yourself using the talent, you'll plant the power of positive thinking in your mind. This poster could also be included in your portfolio.

The Power of Positive Thinking

By picturing yourself using a specific talent, you send yourself a constant positive message about who you are and what you want to do. Great athletes picture themselves making touchdowns or coming in first in a track meet, and this helps them put out the extra effort needed to win. Singers who are struggling to break into the music business picture their names on the cover of a record album, and this helps them stick to the job even when they have no recording contract. To make it through long hours in the laboratory, a scientist might picture himself or herself discovering a cure for a disease. Likewise, job seekers "see" themselves reaching their goals.

This simple technique creates in you a strong urge to succeed. In his book, *Think and Grow Rich,* Napoleon Hill gave many examples of how someone can turn a strong desire or image into reality. Napoleon Hill studied how people became rich and famous. He found that they all used this technique. Most of the people featured in his study began without riches or fame, but they had a strong urge to succeed. This desire became like a huge magnet that attracted others with similar interests. Like them, you might attract other people who can help you move closer to reaching your goals.

How to Make Your Own Talents Poster

1. Study the examples

Look at the talents posters on pages 51 and 52. These posters were created on a computer and printed on a laser printer. If you don't have this equipment, your poster will look more homemade. That's all right, because what's most important is the process of making the poster and using it to represent an opportunity, goal, or dream in your life.

2. Think Like an Advertising Agency

What words or pictures can you use to describe your talents and interests? It doesn't matter which you start with—words or pictures—as long as you eventually combine them in a single poster.

Imagine that you work at an advertising agency. For example, assume you've just finished designing an advertisement and a box for a new cereal. In the ad, you stressed why the cereal would be good to eat and easy to fix. On the front of the box, you used a big picture of someone enjoying the cereal. On the sides, you wrote detailed statements to try to convince customers to buy the new cereal. You described the cereal's ingredients and strong points.

Think of your poster as an advertisement for the purchase of your talents. You are trying to convince the buyer to invest in your product. In this case, the "buyer" is really you. The poster will be used to convince your entire being that you are going to fulfill an important dream of someday using your talents. To make the message convincing, you'll have to write some persuasive "copy" to describe your experiences, skills, passions, and talents. You can even throw in a dash of humor to sweeten the message.

3. Combine Pictures, Words, and Headlines

Now combine your words and pictures on paper. What if you don't have access to a computer? Use a typewriter or do the printing by hand. Your poster doesn't have to look exactly like the examples. Just come up with something that's meaningful for you.

Put a headline at the top of the page and a picture in the upper half. How can you get big headline letters? Use rub-on letters, cut-out letters from newspaper headlines, ask a calligrapher to make headlines, or use a computer.

Good luck! Be creative, be wild...enjoy this project.

Career Goal:

CARPENTRY AND CONSTRUCTION

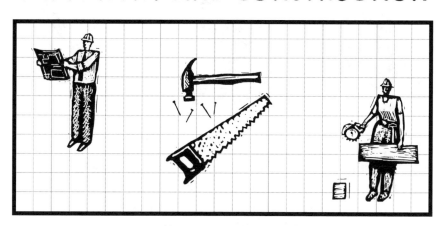

I can build to specification precisely

UNLIMITED ENERGY

Can Handle Many Responsibilities
While going to school, held part-time job and participated in varsity basketball. Was able to maintain grade point average of 3.0 (on a 4.0 scale).

Productivity Is My Game
During the summer, I worked 40–60 hour weeks, maintained my weight training program, and volunteered monthly at the Refugee Center.

SKILLED WORKER

I Believe in a Craftsman's Pride
In woodworking class I earned a grade of "A." Designed and drew scale plans for a complete kitchen, which received first place in statewide competition.

Experienced Carpenter
Assisted finish carpenters as well as rough-in crew in home building. I was called more often than any other summer trainee.

Personal Goal:

Become a Children's Book Author

Editor of School Newspaper

Beginning as a reporter, I advanced to Editor. Our newspaper has won awards statewide and has circulated nationally.

Mastery of Macintosh and IBM Desktop Publishing Software

I have often been asked to help teachers prepare reports, fliers, and brochures. I love to communicate with both words and pictures. I enjoy using clip art to illustrate children's stories I have written.

Early Child Care

I have completed both classes and internships in Early Child Care. I have read over 60 children's books and have written some of my own. The children always ask me to read my works over and over.

Young Author's Publishing Contract

I have been offered a contract to have my book distributed on the Young Author's Network. I will be one of the first people to see my work published and distributed electronically.

How to Use Your Talents Poster

Place your talents poster where you'll see it every day after waking up and before going to bed. Really *look* at your talents poster. Try these suggestions:

1. Close your eyes and picture a place where you could use your talents. *Example:* You see yourself repairing bicycles in a bike shop.

2. Try to see the details of the workplace. *Example:* It's a small shop with two big windows and fluorescent lights. You work near a large tool cabinet. Bikes are stacked behind you. A small desk holds the customer orders. A tape deck plays your favorite music.

3. Try to picture the people around you. *Example:* Your boss stands next to you. A former bike racer, she still rides a lot. This woman is a very easy person to get along with. Even though she likes different kinds of music than you do, she lets you bring in your tapes on Mondays and Fridays.... A person appears at the counter, a young boy waiting for you to straighten the rim on his rear wheel.

4. Picture what you look like and imagine how you feel. *Example:* You're wearing a flannel shirt, old jeans, and a bike-racing hat. A little sweat has collected on your forehead. Your head moves up and down to the music. You hold a stainless-steel spoke wrench in your hand. Your forearm looks strong. You move quickly and gracefully with your hand. You smile because you enjoy your work, your boss, and your life. You have wanted to do this kind of work forever. You feel as if your life's finally making sense.

5. Try to create a powerful feeling inside of you. *Example:* As you see these images in your mind, pay attention to your emotions, especially a strong desire to do a certain kind of work. This desire is like a little voice saying, "I know I would be good at this. I know I'll find an opportunity."

6. End by repeating some of the words or phrases from your Talents Poster. Saying something over and over will help to fix it in your mind. *Examples:* "I am experienced and learn quickly...I am experienced and learn quickly...I am experienced and learn quickly...." Repeat this, gradually lowering your voice until it fades out. Then open your eyes.

Will It Work for You?

Some people wonder if picturing themselves achieving their goals can really change their lives. Opinions vary. If the topic interests you, read on to find out why some people think this technique helps them to become successful. Then make up your own mind.

How It Works

After picturing yourself as the person in your talents poster, you'll have a positive image in your mind. A strong desire in your head and heart will help focus your life around a goal. You'll find yourself talking about your goals to friends and people you meet. Your strong feelings will attract people who have similar thoughts.

This method works because we're all attracted to people who share our interests and enthusiasm. Practicing this technique daily will draw people and opportunities to you. Your strong desire to succeed will start to become a reality. People will say to themselves, "I'll bet that person would do an excellent job at bicycle repair. I'll mention his or her name to my friend who owns a bicycle shop...." We all enjoy helping people who bring a certain energy, joy, and enthusiasm to our lives. Your positive feelings will go out to others like a good TV commercial or public service message.

Give It a Try

What if you've never done this type of exercise before? You might feel unsure about whether it will work for you. That's all right. Try it twice a week for at least three months. If you don't run into opportunity by then, perhaps this technique isn't for you. But don't be surprised if it works!

Write me and let me know how you used your talents poster. I'd also be interested in seeing your talents poster, if you think it's creative. Maybe I could use it in the next version of *Creating Portfolios*. Send your talents poster to me, Martin Kimeldorf, at this address:

Free Spirit Publishing Inc.
217 Fifth Avenue North, Suite 200
Minneapolis, MN 55401-1299

P.S.: If you use this technique to work toward or achieve a life-goal, you might mention this in your portfolio presentation.

Bibliography

Articles and monographs by Judith A. Arter: "Using Portfolios of Student Work in Instruction and Assessment," *Educational Measurement: Issues and Practice,* Spring 1992, pp. 36-44. "Portfolio Resources" (an annotated bibliography of information about portfolios), Northwest Regional Educational Laboratory, 101 S.W. Main, Suite 500, Portland, OR 97204.

Career-Technical Assessment Project (C-TAP) Portfolio Guidebooks (San Francisco: Far West Laboratory for Educational Research and Development, 1993 edition). A comprehensive program which can be used by teachers and schools to help develop a portfolio-assessment system which demonstrates how student's talents translate into career and work world realities. Copies are available at a nominal price. Write to: Far West Laboratory for Educational Research and Development, California Department of Education, 730 Harrison St., San Francisco, CA 94107.

Electronic Job Search Revolution and *Electronic Résumé Revolution* by Joyce Kennedy and Thomas J. Morrow (New York: John Wiley & Sons, Inc., 1994). Learn to glean tips from the emerging online job search culture, which involves résumé databases, employer databases, applicant tracking systems, online want ads, and many other online services. Ultimately, electronic portfolios will probably enter this emerging online labor market.

How To Prepare Your Portfolio by Ed Marquand (New York: Art Direction Book Company, 1981). Originally written for students and artists. Although it emphasizes pre-desktop technology, it includes many good tips about organization and assembly.

Portfolio Information Guide, Employability Skills (Michigan State Board of Education, 1992). Under Catherine Smith, this department has produced excellent materials for the student, teacher, and parent. Be sure to ask to see the "Portfolio Information Guide" and "Parent Information Guide." The portfolio model is based on a survey of the expectations of Michigan's employers. Write to: Michigan Department of Education, Michigan Education Assessment Program, Box 30008, Lansing, MI 48909.

Portfolio News. A quarterly publication that includes articles about portfolios in various disciplines (K-University), book reviews, resources, and listings of portfolio projects around the country. For subscription information, write to: Editor, Portfolio News, Teacher Education Program, University of California, San Diego, 9500 Gilman Dr., La Jolla, CA 92093-0070.

Portfolio Portraits by Donald H. Graves and Bonnie S. Sunstein (Portsmouth, NH: Heinemann Educational Books Inc., 1992). Covers a wide range of portfolio issues and topics; examines classroom practices from elementary school through college; includes individual case studies and an interesting chapter about definitions of the word "portfolio." The opening essay by Donald H. Graves is must reading.

Process and Portfolios in Writing Instruction, edited by Kent Gill (Urbana, IL: National Council of Teachers of English, 1993), and *Portfolios in the Classroom,* edited by Kathleen Yancy (NCTE, 1992). Compilations of ideas from various teachers about using portfolios in the classroom; different models; types of assessments; and the connection between portfolios and good writing.

The ScrapBook Curriculum ToolKit by Emery Roth II. A carefully indexed, 70-page reference book describing the online ScrapBook Writing Project (see page 13). The book includes an overview of the process, step-by-step instructions for various activities and process writing, and technical tips for using America Online efficiently. The work is richly illustrated with numerous examples of students' writings and teacher observations. To acquire a copy, write to: Emery Roth II, 328 Romford Road, Washington, CT 06794 or e-mail him at AFCTooter@aol.com.

Student Portfolios by Laura Grosvenor, et al. (Washington, DC: National Education Association, 1993). The first in a new series of NEA Teacher-to-Teacher Books, published by the NEA Professional Library, presents six first-person stories of classroom teachers using portfolios for both presentation and alternative assessment.

The Walkabout Papers: Challenging Students to Challenge Themselves by Dr. Maurice Gibbons (Vancouver, BC: EduServe Inc., 1990). Describes the "challenge" method of education wherein students develop expertise and confidence in the pursuit of a personally chosen challenge.

What Color Is Your Parachute? by Richard Bolles (Berkeley, CA: Ten Speed Press, 1994). The best selling (and best) book on the topic of "parachuting" onto your best career path. Must reading if you want students to include occupational or career samples in their portfolios.

Write Into a Job by Martin Kimeldorf (Bloomington, IL: Meridian Education Corp., 1990). This book on résumé writing is a natural follow-up to portfolio production. It will be updated and revised by the author pending a new publisher in 1994.

Other Books by the Author

....

Educator's Job Search is a quick-and-easy, step-by-step method for job-hunting teachers. The steps and examples illustrate how to identify marketable skills, network for leads, write effective résumés and letters, prepare for interviews, plan effective follow-up, and more. Write to: National Education Association, 1201 16th St. N.W., Washington, DC 20036.

Job Search Education effectively translates the self-directed job club model into a classroom-tested curriculum. Includes detailed instructions about all phases of job finding: self-assessment, networking, writing letters, collecting important documents, telephoning for job leads, interviewing, etc. Write to: Educational Design, 47 W. 13th, New York, NY 10011.

KIB Writes/KIB Speaks/KIB Reports series by Kids In Between includes ten reproducible units sold individually or as a set. The series takes students from the terrifying first step of starting to write through brainstorming, organizing, drafting and revising. The series also includes power writing, journal writing, creating ads, writing poetry, taking surveys, making reports, speechmaking, script writing, and more. For more information, contact: Kids In Between, P.O. Box 1037, Ballwin, MO 63021; toll-free 1-800-481-2799; *www.kidsinbetween.com*.

Looking for Leisure in All the Right Places is a workbook about expanding leisure opportunities. It helps students focus on healthy choices in a world plagued by drug abuse, unsafe sex, gang affiliation, teen suicide and alienation. After teaching students about the dangers of poor choices, we need to help them discover what they can say "yes" to. It's available as a PDF e-book at PublishingOnline.com *(www.publishingonline.com)* or for more information, write to: 1200 S. 192nd Street, Suite 300, Seattle, WA 98148.

Portfolio Power: The Creative Way to Showcase Your Job Skills and Experience shows that portfolios aren't just for artists and writers anymore. *Portfolio Power* illustrates the many different ways portfolios can be used in a professional career. This important graphical document can be presented on paper, in-person, and over the Internet. It is a highly effective way to visually document your skills, knowledge, and progression in your field. It's available as a PDF e-book at PublishingOnline.com *(www.publishingonline.com)* or for more information, write to: 1200 S. 192nd Street, Suite 300, Seattle, WA 98148.

Work Journal helps students sharpen their critical observation and reflective-thinking habits about the success factors needed on a job. Students analyze employers' personalities and evaluation roles, coworker relationships, stress and humor on the job, and various job survival tactics. Write to: ATC Learning, P.O. Box 43795, Birmingham, AL 35243, or email: atclearning@home.com.

Index

· ·

About the Author

Martin Kimeldorf is the author of over 15 books and reports on the topics of job finding, leisure finding, community service, journal writing, and recreational drama. He holds Bachelor of Science degrees in technology education and liberal arts from Oregon State University and a Master's Degree in special education from Portland State University. He has taught in public schools, prisons, and colleges. He received the Literati Award from the *International Journal of Career Management* for Best Paper of the Year and has won other awards for teaching and playwriting. His hobbies include wood carving, painting, and magic. Martin lives with his wife, Judy, and their dog, Mitzi, in Tumwater, Washington.

Martin has created three portfolios and several scrapbooks on various topics. When looking for work in 1975, he used a teaching portfolio. When showing his paintings in 1993, he created an art portfolio. And when he began his studies of wood carving in the early 1970s, he created a personal portfolio with photos showing his work and the work of other people he admired.

Workshops for Educators

....

Martin Kimeldorf is an experienced public speaker who has provided consultations and workshops for a wide variety of audiences. His workshops for educators include:

- Portfolio Studio
- Résumé Writing
- Job Search Education
- Educator's Job Search Techniques
- wRites of Passage: A Journal Writing Apprenticeship
- Pathways to Leisure Wellness: A Workshop About Balancing Work and Leisure Choices
- Community Service
- Journal Writing in the Workplace
- and others.

For more information about Martin's workshops, write to him c/o Free Spirit Publishing Inc., 217 Fifth Avenue North, Suite 200, Minneapolis, MN 55401-1299.

Other Great Books from Free Spirit

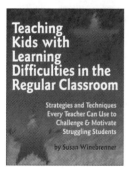
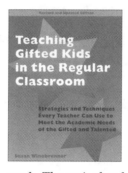

Visit us on the Web!
www.freespirit.com

Stop by anytime to find our Parents' Choice Approved catalog with fast, easy, secure 24-hour online ordering; "Ask Our Authors," where visitors ask questions—and authors give answers—on topics important to children, teens, parents, teachers, and others who care about kids; links to other Web sites we know and recommend; fun stuff for everyone, including quick tips and strategies from our books; and much more! Plus our site is completely searchable so you can find what you need in a hurry. Stop in and let us know what you think!

Just point and click!

Win free books!
As a way of thanking everyone who's made our Web site a success, we often have book giveaways online. Stop by and get in on the action!

new! Get the first look at our books, catch the latest news from Free Spirit, and check out our site's newest features.

contact Do you have a question for us or for one of our authors? Send us an email. Whenever possible, you'll receive a response within 48 hours.

order! Order in confidence! Our secure server uses the most sophisticated online ordering technology available. And ordering online is just one of the ways to purchase our books: you can also order by phone, fax, or regular mail. No matter which method you choose, excellent service is our ultimate goal.

1.800.735.7323 • fax 612.337.5050 • help4kids@freespirit.com